CORAL REEF

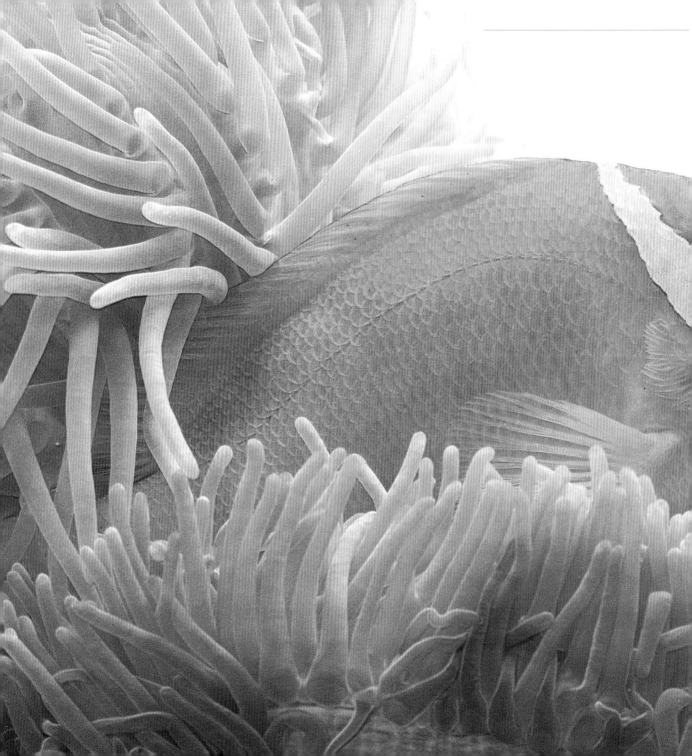

CORAL REEF

PHOTOGRAPHED BY
JANE BURTON

WRITTEN BY
BARBARA TAYLOR

A Dorling Kindersley Book

DK

Dorling Kindersley
LONDON, NEW YORK, SYDNEY, DELHI
PARIS, MUNICH, JOHANNESBURG

Project editor Christiane Gunzi **Project art editor** Val Wright
Editorial assistant Deborah Murrell **Designer** Julie Staniland
Design assistance Nicola Rawson **Production** Louise Barratt
Illustrations Nick Hall, Nick Hewetson **Additional editorial assistance** Jill Somerscales
Animals supplied by Dorking Aquatic Centre **Managing editor** Sophie Mitchell
Managing art editor Miranda Kennedy **U.S. editor** B. Alison Weir
Consultants Paul Clarke, Mandy Holloway, Charles Hussey, Bryan Pitkin, Kathie Way
Coral, p.11 photographed by Linda Pitkin
Endpapers photographed by Henry Ausloos, NHPA

First American Edition, 1992
Paperback Edition, 2000
2 4 6 8 10 9 7 5 3 1
Published in the United States by
Dorling Kindersley Publishing, Inc., 95 Madison Avenue, New York, New York 10016

Copyright © 1992 Dorling Kindersley Ltd., London

Library of Congress Cataloging-in-Publication Data
Taylor, Barbara, 1954-
Coral reef/by Barbara Taylor. – 1st American ed.
p. cm. – (Look closer)
Includes index.
Summary: Examines the variety of life found on coral reefs,
including the sea horse, hermit crab, and sea slug.
ISBN 0-7894-6101-3
1. Coral reef fauna – Juvenile literature. (1.Coral reef animals.)
I. Title. II. Series: Taylor, Barbara, 1954-
Look closer.
QL 125.T39 1992
591.9'1–dc20

Color reproduction by Colourscan, Singapore.
Printed and bound in China by L. Rex Printing Co., Ltd.

For our complete catalog visit
www.dk.com

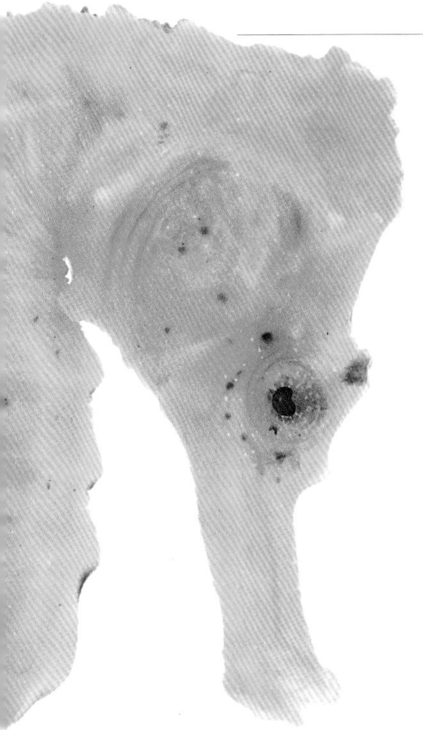

CONTENTS

Life on a coral reef 8

Horse of the sea 10

Reef builders 11

Big blue clam 12

Secondhand home 14

Coral reef friends 16

Shy strawberry 18

Coral reef kaleidoscope 20

Crawling cucumber 22

Top of the class 24

Striped angels 26

Lettuce slug 28

Index and glossary 29

Look for us, and we
will show you the
size of every animal
that you read about
in this book.

The sea horse *(Hippocampus kuda)* is 5 in. long.

LIFE ON A CORAL REEF

CORAL REEFS TEEM WITH a rich variety of wildlife, from spotted shrimps and frilly sea slugs, to giant clams and schools of brightly colored fish. A coral reef takes thousands of years to form. It is built up from the skeletons of tiny animals called corals. Corals can only survive in clean, warm, salty water that is shallow enough to allow sunlight to reach them. Coral reefs all over the world are threatened, mainly because of pollution and overfishing. We must protect the coral reefs if the animals and plants that live on them are to survive.

This clown fish *(Amphiprion* family) is 11/2 in. long.

The giant blue clam *(Tridacna maxima)* is 6 in. across its shell.

The sea slug *(Elysia crispata)* is 1 in. long.

The sea anemone's *(Heteractis malu)* tentacles are 11/4 in. long.

The hermit crab's *(Dardanus megistos)* body and shell is 31/4 in. long.

This clown fish *(Amphiprion* family) is 7 in. long.

The common octopus
(Octopus vulgaris)
is 91/2 in. wide, including
its tentacles.

**The young emperor
angelfish**
*(Pomacanthus
imperator)*
is 21/2 in. long.

The mandarin fish
(Synchiropus splendidus)
is 31/4 in. long.

**The adult emperor
angelfish**
*(Pomacanthus
imperator)*
is 43/4 in. long.

**The strawberry
shrimp**
(Lysmata debelius)
is 11/4 in. long.

A grape coral's
(Plerogyra sinuosa)
tentacle is 21/2 in. long.

The sea cucumber
(Paracumaria group)
is 43/4 in. long.

HORSE OF THE SEA

IT IS HARD TO BELIEVE that the sea horse is a fish. It has a head like a horse, a pouch like a kangaroo, and a tail for holding onto things, like a monkey. A sea horse can change color to match its habitat and hide from enemies. This is useful because it cannot swim fast to escape danger. These shy, peaceful creatures spend most of the day among the coral waiting for food, such as shrimp, to pass within reach. During courtship, sea horses dance with their tails twined together. The female lays her eggs in a pouch on the front of the male's body. The eggs develop inside the pouch and the young emerge after two to seven weeks. As soon as they are born, young sea horses must fend for themselves.

DROPPING ANCHOR

The sea horse uses its strong, supple tail to anchor itself firmly to corals, seaweed, and sponges on the reef. This prevents the sea horse from being thrown around and injured by waves or underwater currents.

The sea horse's eyes move independently, so it can look in two directions at once.

Close up, you can see ridges where the bony plates inside the body join to form the skeleton.

These small fins look like ears. The sea horse flaps them to steer itself through the water.

This transparent fin sweeps back and forth to slowly push the sea horse through the water.

The fin on the back beats as many as 20 to 35 times a second.

To rise up, the sea horse straightens its tail. It curls its tail to sink down.

Its jaws are long and hollow, like a drinking straw.

NOISY EATER

The sea horse has no teeth and swallows its food whole. It sucks up shrimp with its long, hollow jaws, making a clicking noise which can be heard some distance away. Sea horses feed almost all day long. They eat enormous amounts because they have no stomach in which to store food.

GUESS WHAT?

A young sea horse eats as many as 3,500 shrimp in a day and grows more than twice its size in less than a month.

REEF BUILDERS

THESE BEAUTIFUL GRAPE corals may look like unusual plants, but they are really carnivorous (meat-eating) animals. Corals are related to jellyfish and sea anemones. Like them, they use stinging cells to defend themselves and catch their food. A coral colony like this one is made up of hundreds of individual creatures, called polyps. The polyps divide into two over and over again to form exact copies of themselves. They also produce eggs which, when fertilized, develop into larvae. The larvae swim around in the sea until they reach a suitable spot to settle down and develop into adults. Over thousands of years, the skeletons of dead corals build up on top of each other to form a reef.

DEADLY HARPOONS

Corals cannot move, so they rely on the movement of the water to bring their food to them. The poisonous tentacles paralyze the prey, then pass it to the mouth. Each tentacle of this grape coral is about the size of your finger. It feeds at night, on microscopic animals.

The polyp can close up and pull its tentacles back inside its body for protection.

When this coral polyp is open, you can see its many smooth tentacles.

BIG BLUE CLAM

THIS COLORFUL giant clam is a soft-bodied animal that lives inside a strong, hard shell. The shell is made of two halves that can open and close. A clam opens its shell to feed and shuts it tight when threatened. Growing in the clam's body are millions of tiny seaweed plants called algae. These plants absorb some of the clam's waste products and, in return, the clam feeds on some of the algae. It also eats microscopic plants called plankton that drift past in the sea water. Clams develop from tiny eggs that hatch into larvae. The larvae swim around for about nine days, then settle down on the reef to grow into adults. Giant clams do not move once they are mature, and they sometimes grow as large as one yard across.

SUPER SIPHON

Clams have no head, so they cannot breathe and feed in the same way as other animals do. Instead, they have two openings called siphons. A small siphon allows water full of oxygen and food to pass into the body. The large siphon squirts waste products out of the body.

Waste products leave the body through this large siphon.

LIVING LARDER

The green patches on the clam are colonies (groups) of algae. Algae lives in the part called the mantle, which is the frilly layer between the clam's soft body and the hard shell. The algae grows and multiplies throughout the clam's life, so the clam always has a good source of food.

The two sides of the mantle join together so that the clam's body is completely enclosed and cannot be seen by predators.

Ridges and grooves on the shell make it strong. They also help to disguise the clam when it closes its shell.

GUESS WHAT?

Blue clams like this one can live for 100 years. During their lives, they sometimes make pearls as big as golf balls. This process may take 10 years or more.

HINGED HOME

The clam first makes its shell from chemicals in the water, then the mantle gradually adds layers of chalk to the shell to make it grow bigger. The shell supports and protects the clam's soft body. The matching halves are joined together with a hinge, and strong muscles close them together for protection. The body of the clam is joined to the shell by muscles.

Simple eyes are all the clam needs.

Algae grows in the large, fleshy mantle. It produces its own food by using the energy in sunlight.

EYES EVERYWHERE
Rows of sensitive eyes along the edge of the mantle can detect changes in light and shadow. This helps the clam to see predators in time to heave its shell slowly shut.

There is a siphon that sucks in water.

SECONDHAND HOME

THIS EXTRAORDINARY CRAB spends its life inside another animal's shell. Hermit crabs like this one protect the soft rear part of their body, called the abdomen, by living in the empty shells of whelks and other sea snails. The coiled abdomen fits inside the shell, and a hook on the end helps the crab keep a firm grip on it. The crab can stretch its legs out of the shell to pull itself along. The hermit crab takes its home with it wherever it goes. When the crab grows too big for one shell, it simply moves to a larger one. Female hermit crabs lay eggs, which they carry around on one side of the abdomen. The eggs hatch into tiny larvae that drift in the sea with the plankton. Eventually the larvae settle down to become adults and find a shell-home of their own.

Bright dots on the body help disguise the crab on the coral reef.

Special hairs called setae help the crab to feel its way around. They also detect the movements of predators or food in the water.

At the first sign of danger, the crab quickly pulls its whole body back inside this conch shell for protection.

NEW CLOTHES FOR OLD

The hard outer skin, called the exoskeleton, is on the front part of the body. It does not expand as the crab grows. Instead, the crab molts its exoskeleton from time to time. A soft new exoskeleton grows beneath the old one, which splits so that the crab can pull itself out. The new exoskeleton takes time to harden.

GUESS WHAT?
There are many different kinds of hermit crabs. Some are only the size of a pea, and others are as big as your hand.

HOUSE HUNTING

Hermit crabs must search for an empty shell that is the right size. Before moving in, they investigate and explore the shell with their claws to see if it is large enough. Some hermit crabs live inside tubes in coral or wood instead of shells.

Large eyes
peer out from
the ends of
long stalks.

The antennae
are sensitive
to touch.

Feathery
mouthparts
are used for
feeding.

MUD, GLORIOUS MUD
The hermit crab uses its
mouthparts to sift through
sand or mud for food
particles. It also scavenges
for dead animals or plants,
and sometimes it even
catches small fish.

CLEVER CLAWS
Hermit crabs have ten legs. The
front two legs are a pair of large
pincers or nippers, used for
feeding, cleaning, and defense.
When a hermit crab senses
danger, it quickly draws
back inside the shell and
seals the entrance with
its hard claws.

The exoskeleton is
very hard so the
legs are jointed.
This allows
them to bend.

Huge claws are used for
fighting, catching food,
and barricading the crab's
shell from attackers.

CORAL REEF FRIENDS

CLOWN FISH LIVE ON the coral reef in harmony with another creature called the sea anemone. Sea anemones are related to corals and jellyfish, and they have poisonous tentacles for stinging prey. At the first sign of danger, a clown fish darts into the anemone's tentacles for safety. To protect itself from the poison, the fish covers itself with a layer of slimy mucus. The anemone also produces mucus to protect itself from its own sting. In return for the protection of the tentacles, the fish frightens enemies away from the anemone. The clown fish also lays its eggs and rears its young among the tentacles. Some sea anemones lay eggs, too. Others make smaller versions of themselves by dividing their bodies into two.

GUESS WHAT?
Clown fish have never been seen living without sea anemones, but sea anemones can survive without clown fish.

TERRIBLE TENTACLES
The sea anemone grabs small creatures floating past in the water with its stinging tentacles. It also catches young fish and shrimps. The tentacles pass the prey down to the mouth opening, then spread out again to catch more food.

Tentacles grasp prey and push it toward the mouth opening.

CLOWN COSTUME
The clown fish's bright colors mean that it cannot easily hide from its enemies. But it can escape by swimming among the tentacles of the anemone, which makes it hard to catch. The colors and patterns of the fish may also warn predators of the anemone's poisonous tentacles, and help keep both animals safe.

The large eyes watch for danger.

Hundreds of stinging tentacles catch food.

The clown fish's mouth has a hard jaw for nibbling at algae on the coral reef. It also feeds on tiny creatures called plankton.

The base of the anemone's body is attached to a rock for support.

Side fins are used for steering and changing direction.

SHY STRAWBERRY

THIS STRAWBERRY SHRIMP is one of many kinds of tiny, brightly colored shrimps that live on the coral reef. Strawberry shrimp are very shy and hide in natural crevices in the coral or dig burrows in the sand. A strong exoskeleton helps to protect the soft body. Shrimp have paddle-like back legs called swimmerets on the abdomen, which help them to swim fast. Female strawberry shrimp carry their eggs on the swimmerets. A sticky cement holds the eggs in place while they develop. After a few weeks, the eggs hatch into larvae and swim away from their mother. Eventually, the larvae change into tiny versions of the adults and settle down on the reef to make homes of their own.

The shrimp uses its walking legs to preen (clean) its antennae.

BALANCING ACT
At the base of the antennae is a special organ called a statocyst, which helps the shrimp to balance. This organ is like a sack containing sand or grit. Each time the shrimp moves, the grit moves inside the sack. Cells in the sack send information to the brain, so the shrimp can determine its position in the water.

There is a special organ inside here for balancing.

Each antenna is made up of lots of segments so it can bend.

CLEANING SERVICE
The shrimp strains particles of food from the water with its fringed mouthparts. Strawberry shrimp are known as cleaners because they use their mouthparts to remove parasites from the scales of fish. They also scavenge for dead animal or plant remains and catch living prey, such as plankton.

The two pairs of antennae detect chemicals in the water and help the shrimp find food.

If the shrimp loses one of its claws, a new one grows to replace it.

The shrimp uses its claws, called chelipeds, to grasp or pick up food and also for digging in the sand.

GUESS WHAT?
During the day, "cleaning" shrimp like this one often gather together to form special "cleaning stations." Fish visit them so that the shrimp can clean them of parasites.

This jagged point on the carapace is called a rostrum. It juts out to protect the front of the head.

The two large compound eyes detect movement in the water.

The top part of the exoskeleton, called the carapace, protects the front of the body, called the thorax.

The shrimp's bright colors help fish recognize that this is a "cleaning" shrimp.

NEW SKIN FOR OLD
Strawberry shrimp grow rapidly in short bursts because they can only increase in size when they molt. They usually eat the old exoskeleton each time they molt because it contains nutritious salts. The soft new exoskeleton takes time to stretch and harden, so strawberry shrimp hide away from enemies, such as fish and crabs, until their new armor is strong.

Close up, you can see many tiny hair-like setae covering the body.

A flexible, segmented abdomen allows the shrimp to swim backward very rapidly.

Strawberry shrimp can walk slowly over the coral reef on their four pairs of long front legs.

CORAL REEF KALEIDOSCOPE

THE BRILLIANTLY COLORED mandarin fish lives near the bottom of the sea. It spends most of its time hidden in crevices or cracks in the coral reef. The mandarin fish feeds on smaller fish and other creatures that swim or float past it in the water. It also nibbles at the algae on the coral reef with its hard mouth. The bold patterns on its skin help to protect the fish from enemies, by warning them of the bad-tasting mucus that its body produces. The mandarin fish can also deter larger fish from attacking it by raising the long spine on its back. This trick makes the fish appear larger than it really is.

There are no eyelids or tear ducts on the eyes. The sea water cleans the eyes instead.

The small, downturned mouth is a good shape for nibbling food from the coral reef.

Bony covers protect the gills, which take in oxygen from the water.

This long, pointed spine is the first ray of the front fin on the fish's back. These back fins are called dorsal fins.

Both eyes stick out so the fish can see in front and to the sides. Mandarin fish can see things in color.

The tail fin moves from side to side to push and steer the fish through the water.

This ventral fin, together with the dorsal fin, helps the fish to stay upright in the water.

SIXTH SENSE

Like all fish, the mandarin fish has a line of pores, or holes, called the lateral line, along each side of the body. The lateral line contains special sense organs which detect movements and pressure changes in the water. These help the fish to find its way around and to sense danger - or a possible meal.

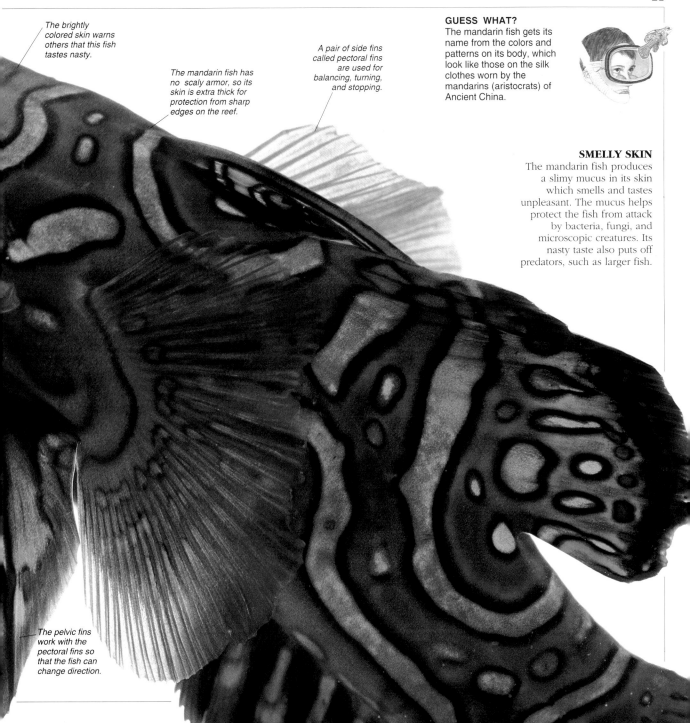

The brightly colored skin warns others that this fish tastes nasty.

The mandarin fish has no scaly armor, so its skin is extra thick for protection from sharp edges on the reef.

A pair of side fins called pectoral fins are used for balancing, turning, and stopping.

GUESS WHAT?
The mandarin fish gets its name from the colors and patterns on its body, which look like those on the silk clothes worn by the mandarins (aristocrats) of Ancient China.

SMELLY SKIN
The mandarin fish produces a slimy mucus in its skin which smells and tastes unpleasant. The mucus helps protect the fish from attack by bacteria, fungi, and microscopic creatures. Its nasty taste also puts off predators, such as larger fish.

The pelvic fins work with the pectoral fins so that the fish can change direction.

CRAWLING CUCUMBER

SAUSAGE-SHAPED SEA CUCUMBERS crawl over the coral reef on their tube feet, picking up particles of food with their sticky tentacles. These extraordinary animals are related to starfish and sea urchins and have lived on Earth for millions of years. The sea cucumber has no head, just a mouth at one end and an opening for waste removal at the other end. Their bodies are bendable and can easily change color and shape. Some sea cucumbers can produce poisonous, sticky threads to trap enemies. Sea cucumbers lay eggs that develop into larvae. The larvae are small and transparent and drift along in the sea, eventually settling down to grow into adults. Adult sea cucumbers lay thousands of eggs because many of the larvae will be eaten and only a few survive to become adults.

FEATHERY FEELERS
Around the mouth, there are many large, feathery tentacles. They are covered with a sticky substance called mucus. The tentacles feel for tiny plants and animals on the coral reef and the sea cucumber sucks the food off the tentacles with its fleshy lips.

GUESS WHAT?
To save itself, a sea cucumber can split its body wall and push out some of its internal organs in order to distract attackers. The sea cucumber will then regrow new body parts in a few weeks.

This opening, called the anus, gets rid of waste materials. The sea cucumber also uses it when it is breathing.

The feathery shape of the tentacles helps them catch as much food as possible.

Particles of food catch on the sticky substance called mucus which covers each tentacle.

Sea cucumbers can pull these tentacles back inside the body to protect them.

The mouth is in the middle of the tentacles.

The tough, spiny skin discourages enemies from eating the sea cucumber.

Suckers on the ends of the tube feet grip onto rocks as the sea cucumber walks.

WALKING ON THE WATER

Many sea cucumbers have rows of brightly colored tube feet along the sides of their bodies. Water fills the tube feet so that they become stiff and work like levers to push the sea cucumber along over the rocks. Suckers on the ends of the feet grip onto rocks and other slippery surfaces.

Each tube foot is full of water.

TOP OF THE CLASS

OCTOPUSES ARE CLEVER animals that can learn and remember things. They are shy and spend most of their time shuffling around on the coral reef or hiding inside their home, which they build from a pile of stones. This common octopus sometimes lurks inside coral caves and attacks crabs and shellfish as they pass by. Octopuses are related to mollusks such as clams, but they do not have a shell and they can swim much faster than most shellfish. A female octopus lays long strings of eggs and hangs them from the roof of her home. She keeps the eggs clean and guards them so carefully that she does not have time to feed herself. After about six weeks, the eggs hatch into tiny octopuses. Soon afterward, the female octopus dies of starvation.

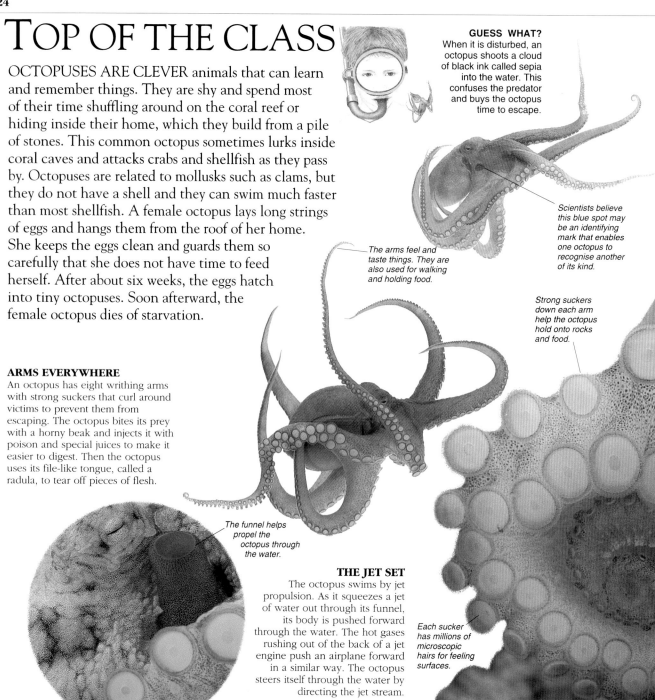

GUESS WHAT?
When it is disturbed, an octopus shoots a cloud of black ink called sepia into the water. This confuses the predator and buys the octopus time to escape.

Scientists believe this blue spot may be an identifying mark that enables one octopus to recognise another of its kind.

The arms feel and taste things. They are also used for walking and holding food.

Strong suckers down each arm help the octopus hold onto rocks and food.

ARMS EVERYWHERE
An octopus has eight writhing arms with strong suckers that curl around victims to prevent them from escaping. The octopus bites its prey with a horny beak and injects it with poison and special juices to make it easier to digest. Then the octopus uses its file-like tongue, called a radula, to tear off pieces of flesh.

The funnel helps propel the octopus through the water.

THE JET SET
The octopus swims by jet propulsion. As it squeezes a jet of water out through its funnel, its body is pushed forward through the water. The hot gases rushing out of the back of a jet engine push an airplane forward in a similar way. The octopus steers itself through the water by directing the jet stream.

Each sucker has millions of microscopic hairs for feeling surfaces.

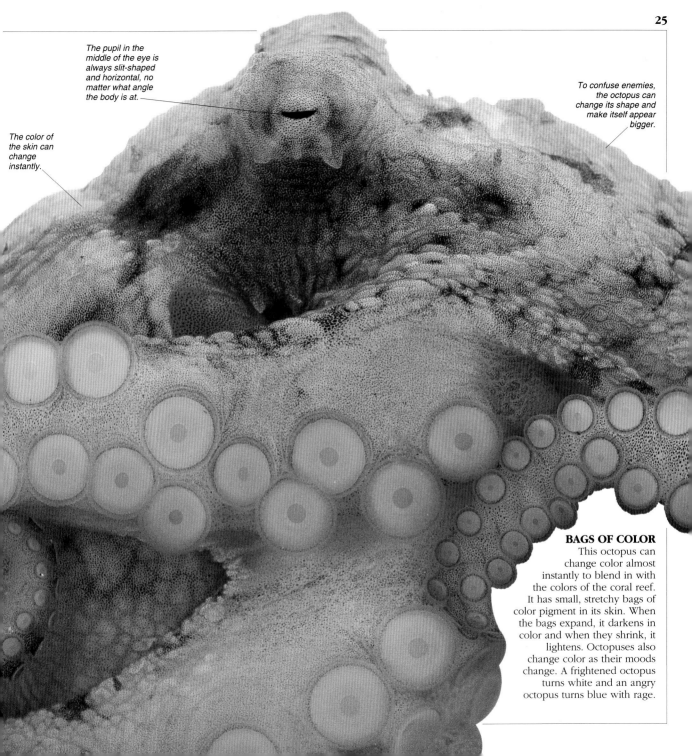

The pupil in the middle of the eye is always slit-shaped and horizontal, no matter what angle the body is at.

To confuse enemies, the octopus can change its shape and make itself appear bigger.

The color of the skin can change instantly.

BAGS OF COLOR

This octopus can change color almost instantly to blend in with the colors of the coral reef. It has small, stretchy bags of color pigment in its skin. When the bags expand, it darkens in color and when they shrink, it lightens. Octopuses also change color as their moods change. A frightened octopus turns white and an angry octopus turns blue with rage.

STRIPED ANGELS

THE EMPEROR ANGELFISH hovers in the water near small caves in the coral reef so that it can shoot inside if it senses danger. Its flat body allows it to slip easily through narrow gaps in the coral. This agile fish spends most of the day nibbling at sponges on the reef. Once two angelfish have mated, they remain together for the rest of their lives. The pair live in their own territory, a small patch of the reef which they defend against other angelfish. The female lays eggs which are fertilized by the male. The eggs float in the sea, away from the reef and the many enemies that might eat them. Larvae hatch out of the eggs, and eventually change into little fish and find a new coral reef.

COLORFUL SIGNALS

The vibrant colors and patterns of this adult emperor angelfish help it recognize others of its own kind. Colors can also attract a mate, and may become brighter in the breeding season. Angelfish usually live in water that is at least 48 feet deep. Their bright colors show up well in the dim light.

There is one eye on each side of the head for good all-round vision.

This spine below the gill cover can lock the fish into a crevice so that an enemy can't pull it out backward.

The strong teeth inside the mouth pull pieces of sponge, coral, and microscopic plants called algae from the reef.

The winglike pectoral fins balance and turn the fish.

The tail fin is called the caudal fin. It pushes the fish along and helps it steer.

SCHOOL UNIFORM
Young emperor angelfish
have blue bodies with white
circles. They often swim in
groups, called schools.Their
uniform appearance helps
protect them from attack by
the adults. The colors of the
young fish are very different
from those of the adults,
and they change gradually
as the fish mature.

GUESS WHAT?
Large adult emperor
angelfish can make a
loud thumping noise
which may startle a
diver. Scientists are not
sure how the fish
produce this sound.

*These light-colored
rings attract predators
to the fish's tail rather
than its head. If the
attacker falls for the
decoy, the angelfish's
head is safe.*

*Close-up, you can
see the overlapping
scales that protect
the body.*

*The dark blue
color and light
pattern help
disguise the young
fish from enemies.*

*This narrow
snout can
reach into
crevices in
the coral*

LETTUCE SLUG

SEA SLUGS ARE RELATED to garden snails, but they have no shell to protect their soft bodies. Most sea slugs have very special diets. Some eat only a few types of sponge, while others feed on coral or even other sea slugs. This lettuce slug feeds on tiny green coral reef plants called algae. Like snails, sea slugs scrape up food with their strong jaws and a special tongue called a radula, which works like a nail file. Sometimes they mix up the food with slimy mucus and suck it up instead. Each sea slug is both male and female at the same time. This makes it easier for them to find a mate and it means that every sea slug can lay eggs. The eggs hatch into larvae that swim around until they find a good place to settle down and grow into adults.

GUESS WHAT?
Some kinds of sea slugs steal poisonous stinging cells from the sea anemones that they feed on and use them for their own defense!

This frilly edge on the body takes in oxygen and absorbs sunlight.

The bright green color indicates that this slug eats tiny green plants called algae.

The soft body has no shell for protection.

A sea slug crawls over the slippery seaweed on its flat, slimy foot.

TERRIBLE TASTE
Lettuce slugs may look like a tasty salad, but they have special glands in their skin that produce a bad-tasting substance. This discourages predators from eating them.

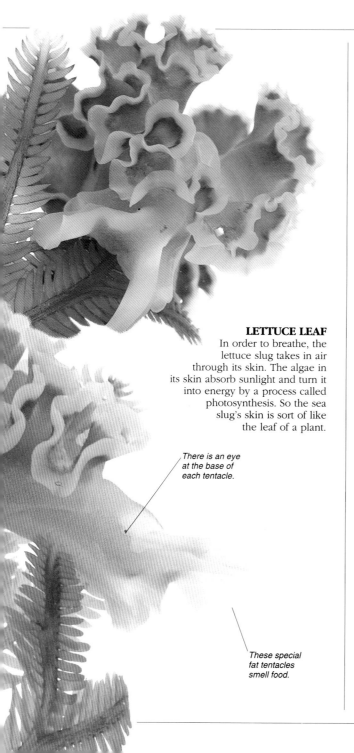

LETTUCE LEAF
In order to breathe, the lettuce slug takes in air through its skin. The algae in its skin absorb sunlight and turn it into energy by a process called photosynthesis. So the sea slug's skin is sort of like the leaf of a plant.

There is an eye at the base of each tentacle.

These special fat tentacles smell food.

INDEX

Abdomen 14, 19
algae 12, 13, 28
angelfish, emperor 9, 26-27
antennae (feelers) 15, 18

Balancing 18, 20, 21, 26
blue clam 8, 12-13
breathing 11, 12, 13, 22, 29
breeding *see each animal*
bubble coral 11

Chalk 12
clam, giant 8, 12-13
claws 15, 18
cleaner shrimp *see strawberry shrimp*
clown fish 8, 16
color
      changing 10, 22, 25, 27
      for recognition 19, 24, 26
      to attract 26, 27
      to disguise 10, 14, 27
      to warn 16, 20
corals 8, 11
courtship dance, sea horse's 10
crab, hermit 8, 14-15

Eggs *see each animal*
emperor angelfish 9, 26-27
enemies, dealing with *see each animal*
exoskeleton 14, 15, 18, 19
eyes, eyesight *see each animal*

Feeding *see each animal*
feet, tube 22, 23
fins 10, 16, 20, 21, 26
foot, sea slug's 28
funnel, water 24

Gills 20, 26
grape coral 9, 11

Hairs 14, 19, 24
hermit crab 8, 14-15

Jaws 10, 28
jet propulsion 24

Larva *see each animal*
legs 14, 15, 18, 19
lettuce slug 8, 28-29
lifespan, blue clam's 12

Mandarin fish 9, 20-21
molting 14, 19

mouth 16, 20, 22, 23, 26
mouthparts 15, 18
mucus 16, 20, 21, 22, 28
muscles, clam's 12

Octopus 9, 24-25

Pearls 12
photosynthesis 29
pincers *see claws*
plankton 12
poison, injecting 24
poisonous
      stinging cells 11, 28
      tentacles 11, 16-17
      threads 22
polyps, coral 11
pouch, sea horse's 10

Reef building 8, 11

Scales, transparent 27
sea anemone 8, 16-17
sea cucumber 9, 22-23
sea horse 8, 10-11
sea slug 8, 28-29
sepia (black ink) 24
shell
      hinged 12
      moving 14
shrimps 9, 18-19
shyness 18, 24
size, changing 20, 22, 25
skeleton 10-11
      outer *see exoskeleton*
skin *see each animal*
slime *see mucus*
slugs 8, 28-29
snout, angelfish's 27
spines 20, 23, 26
stinging cells 11, 28
strawberry shrimp 9, 18-19
suckers 23, 24
swimming *see each animal*

Tail, sea horse's 10
tail fin 20, 27
taste, unpleasant 21, 28
tentacles 22, 23, 29
      poisonous 11, 16-17
thorax, strawberry shrimp's 19
tongue 24, 28

Walking 22, 23, 28

GLOSSARY

Abdomen *the rear part of the body*
Algae *simple plants such as seaweed*
Antennae *a pair of feelers*
Carapace *part of an exoskeleton or shell*
Carnivorous *meat-eating*
Exoskeleton *a tough covering on the body, made of a substance called chitin*
Larva *the young, grub-like stage of an animal such as an insect*
Mandibles *jaws*
Microscopic *too small to see without a microscope*
Mollusk *a soft-bodied animal which often has a shell, such as a snail or slug*
Molt *to shed the skin or exoskeleton*
Mucus *a slimy, often poisonous substance which certain animals produce*

Parasite *a plant or animal which lives in or on another living thing*
Photosynthesis *the use of sunlight by plants to produce the energy to grow*
Plankton *microscopic sea creatures and plants*
Polyps *the tiny animals whose skeletons make up the coral reef*
Predator *a meat-eating hunter*
Prehensile tail *a tail which can grasp hold of things*
Radula *a file-like tongue*
Setae *special hairs on the body*
Tentacles *flexible feelers for touching, feeding, or smelling*
Thorax *the middle part of the body, containing the heart and lungs*